The Expanded Gateway Vol. 2
Wisdom for the Awakened Consciousness

By

Elizabeth Saenz

And the Fairies

Ciernan ~
Your expansion is your destiny. Allow it to unfold.
~ Elizabeth

Copyright © 2013 Elizabeth Saenz

All rights reserved.

ISBN: 1494268566
ISBN-13: 978 - 1494268565

THIS BOOK IS FOR:

My many friends and followers on Facebook, Twitter, the Fairies and Me Blog, and in real face to face time. Thank you for all the support and belief in magic over the years.

CONTENTS

	Acknowledgments	i
1	Fairy Wisdom	3
2	E.L.F.E. symbol	19
3	Fairy Wisdom pt.2	25
4	Manifesting Exercises	43
5	Fairy Wisdom pt. 3	49

THANK YOU

To my amazing Husband, Ryan Saenz, our beautiful children, Alex, Lucas, and Tori, The Fairies, My dear friends, Kristin Ford, Erik Nielsen, Llynya Carey, Ame Seelow, and Red McNally for helping me stay sane in a crazy world and encouraging me to speak my truth. I love you all!

Fairy Wisdom

Watching humanity sometimes is like watching the great master violin player walk around in beggar's clothing. Not playing a violin. Not sharing its gifts with the world. Not taking care and honoring the talent that lays there.

We offer you the violin. Play it! Bring all your talent forward to the earth and see what an amazing talented being you are by just naturally being you, this highly evolved being called human.

All events are an opportunity. They lead you to growth, clarity, choices, and options. When you experience an Earth shaking event you may judge it as a tragedy or a miracle. You can judge it how ever you want, it will still be an opportunity. Open to your path and stop judging the tragedy. Stop resisting the catalyst that will launch you into your next phase of life. You must surrender to the flow of your path and trust all the events are leading you to your destiny. Remember your destiny is not a destination but a series of events you experience.

When a snake sheds its skin or a caterpillar turns to a butterfly they know a very important trick; you have to rest in between each step. Clarity, rest, release, rest, transform, rest, step forward, rest. Rest does not mean you have to stop and be absolutely still, though it may be good for you to do that too. Rest can be play, which rests the spirit. Rest can be a resting of the mind and the constant running you are doing in there. Rest can be laughing till you cry or crying till you laugh. Rest could mean letting yourself off the hook for something you are "suppose to" do and instead taking the "easy way" or shortcut. You do not just have permission to rest but it is a mandatory requirement for your soul's evolution.

There are many of you who think it is unsafe to open your heart all the way; that this will make you vulnerable, weak, and open for attack, disappointment, and hurt. That is because you think opening your heart is like opening the door to a big empty house. NO! Opening your heart is like busting open a dam allowing the river to flow and flood where it has been drought. The power of love flowing from you when your heart is open is like a Giant waterfall spilling out and joining 'The One'. There is no need to guard and protect when you are in that space of true powerful love.

This is not just romantic love, but the love for life, the universe, the planet, and EVERYTHING. When you open your heart you explode with love, sending it into, and all over, everything around you. That is what you fear, not the vulnerability but the power.

There are no villains or evil doers to fight. There is just fear and wounds of the heart that can be dissolved with love and compassion. Take this time to reflect on where you still feel hurt and love that part of yourself. Look for those around you that are having trouble and love them in what ever seems the healthiest way. Mostly this is a reminder to focus love on the children in your life. Children hold the keys to joy, wonder, and love. Help them remember that, honor them, and give them the space to shine.

Humanity needs to remember they are magical beings who can create amazing experiences. When you focus on fear and worry you can create that fear and worry ten fold. This is not a bad thing. Humanity needs to face their fears and worries and experience them to realize they are more then these fears and worries. Too often you tell yourself that if X or Y happened then that is it. It would be the end of you, your life, or your existence. But we promise you that when X or Y happens you will rise above it. It will not be the same experience you created in your head. As humanity keeps facing their fears they realize that no matter what happens they will go on. Life will keep evolving and changing as you do. Some events may bring an end to the way you are but if your life changes that dramatically you will see it is for the better. Let these current events strip you down to the beautiful Divine light love core of your being. When you stand in this energy nothing can threaten you, because you know your connection, purpose, and value.

Humanity is preparing for a massive shift of consciousness. This last decade has been a slow turning of the wheel that gradually gained speed with every turn. You are now going at a very fast pace. It is time for you to surrender to the flow but consciously move with it. Do not allow yourself to just be pulled along or to resist it. You must speak your truth and be clear about the experience you wish to create. Then detach from the details of how. Then detach from what form you believe it should manifest in. Then detach from your ego's idea that it has any control over your path. Accept that not everyone you have known and cared for will be joining you on this ride. Accept that the world is in the midst of huge change which means you are experiencing the chaos of the shift. Accept that no matter what you perceive and judge is happening; it is all Divine, and perfect, and part of your highest good, and the experience that will bring you a step closer to your next goal. You are being handed the sword of your power to wield. It is your choice to grasp it. It is your choice to use it. It is your choice to align with the light of the One and your Authentic self. Otherwise you continue to create struggle by denying yourself. The easiest and softest way is to stop pretending that you can contain the limitless magical being that is you in your limited physical reality and form.

You need to stop perceiving your life as a to-do list and start seeing the journey and the many phases you have been through. Truly look at what you have done or 'been through' the last ten years. Even though at times you feel stuck or stagnant you can look back and see the shifts and the Divine timing of it all.

You forget about the agreement and exchange. You are as much a part of the flow of money as anyone else. You are just as much a part of the exchange as anyone else. This means you receive and give. You must do both. Money can be held as an abstract concept and you can let go of it. It also can be held as a part of your nature. It is made from paper and metals and, even in electronic form, is energy.

You can choose to be a part of the flow, of its natural circulation. A lot of you struggle in a space where you long for it and resist it at the same time. Relax into the concept of money as if it is the same as flowers that grow naturally all around you. You do not own those flowers but you can pick them. You can enjoy them from a distance and you are a part of their eco system no matter how much interaction you choose to have.

When you see animals in the food chain Humanity refers to them as hunter and prey. There seems to be a concept of an animal that is filled with hunger and pushed into a frenzy of killing till it is satiated. You may have also heard it explained as a calculating killer that is able to take down an opponent no matter how hard it tries to escape. Yes there is a conflict of life and death and struggle between animals but Humanity is interpreting these actions through their own perspective. This dance that the animal kingdom has engaged in is that of an intense tango. There is always an agreement between the animals. They understand the cycle of life and nature and accept their part in that flow. Even if it is rabbit against clover, the agreement has been made and energies exchanged accordingly. Humans have taken themselves out of this flow and exchange.

Remember the veil is a creation of Humanity to know how to shift their focus from their reality to another. What is the most important thing for you to know at this time is that all of us beings are assisting in this ascension; consciously or not. We are as much a part of the ascension as you are. First let us define ascension from our perspective. It is the natural evolution of energy and/or a being into a pure form of itself. This is not a lessening, or releasing, it is a shift and integration. Think of a frog moving from tadpole to fully formed frog. As a frog moves through its many stages it needs the waters and plants that surround it to help with its process. Likewise the water and plants are shifted by being a part of the process.

We also wish Humanity to open to the solution of love. When pondering a decision pick the choice that feels the most loving especially for yourself. When you feel stuck, or you can't find an answer, send love energy out into the world or perform a random act of love and let the universe bring the answer to you. When you love, love, love then love, love, love will be returned. Express your love in what ever ways feel fitting in the moment.

Step into your Power, into your fierceness, and to do it all in a gentle way! It does not have to be the conflict of energies that it has been in the past. It does not have to be a power struggle nor will it be a struggle for authority over or power over others. It will be like a giant exhale as you relax into yourself. It will be like peeling off an old tight costume and running naked and free through the fields. A diamond sparkles the best when it is brought into sunlight and the whole world can see it!
Allow yourself to step into the light and Shine!

Wisdom for the Awakened Cosciouness

The Expanded Gateway Vol. 2

E.L.F.E. (Eternal Love Force Energy) Symbol

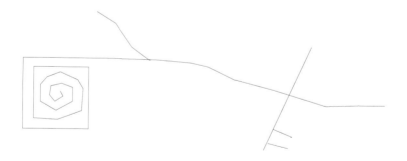

If you have read any of my other books or used my oracle deck then you will have seen this symbol multiple times.

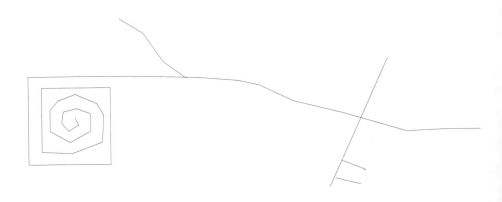

I have been asked what this symbol is and where it came from many times. I usually just give a simple answer like "It was symbol given to me by The Fairies." and leave it at that. There is actually a bit of a story behind it and a lot of information about it. I've decided to share it with you here and hope others can find ways to use it or gain something from the information.

The Eternal Love Force Energy Symbol, or E.L.F.E. as I call it, came to me in a vision years ago. I had been a Reiki Master/Teacher for a couple years. People occasionally receive extra symbols or new symbols after they become a Reiki Master/Teacher. I had been open to this idea but was not looking for it. So, there I was in 2005 doing a meditation just to get centered. This was after reading a magical book that was centered around the Celtic path, which is a spiritual path I resonate with, and I wanted to ask the Fairies about it. When I tuned in I was shone the E.L.F.E. symbol. They showed me the merkaba, or six pointed star, also. Then they said these are healing symbols.

The star was the six steps of healing. These steps are observe, acknowledge, accept, release, love, and grow. First you observe what is not serving you (or the wounding). Then acknowledge its lesson (or existence). Next accept the way it is now is completely Divine and perfect. Release that which no longer serves you. Love yourself and everything the way it is. Then you have no choice but to grow from the experience.

The star represented feelings and abstract thought. The E.L.F.E. symbol represents the physical form and the magical world. The different sections representing different energies. The first section is the spiral that starts circular and becomes squared.

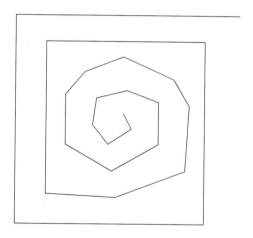

This is the inner physical world that moves out and affects the outer physical world. That can mean many things; feelings and emotions creating physical experiences, thoughts and subconscious thoughts creating physical reality, or the Divine self expressing through the physical self. This symbol is also a map for a vision journey. When using it this way you start at the center of the spiral and follow the line as a path out till you get to the next section. This section is the beginning of the straighter path and the little "tail". It looks like this:

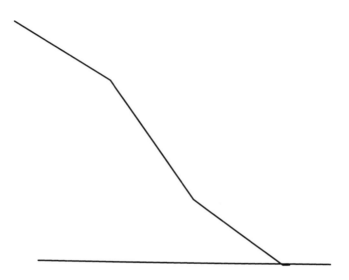

It represents where the light touches the Earth. This is the horizon, the place between worlds, or where the idea becomes manifest. I like to see it as the Divine power flowing into the physical plane. The long path or line is the Earth realm and the physical space we exist in. It also can represent the path you are currently walking or a life path. When using the symbol as a vision journey this part is where you path will take form and you will see the "light line" as light flowing in. I sometimes experience this like a waterfall of light that I walk through. I then follow the path to the rest of the symbol. This path can be just light, water, fire, stones, dirt, or anything else you can think of. Let your path appear to you.

The last section looks like a crossroads, which it kind of is.

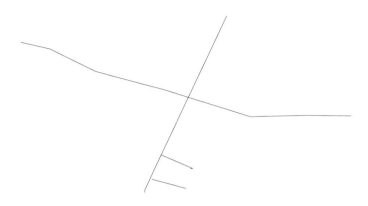

This is the Gateway point. This can represent the gateway between the physical and non-physical, or the gateway between soul and body, or just about any other gateway you can think of. This works really well to intend as a gateway between our realm and the Fairy Realm. The long line is a continuation of the walking path in the vision journey. It also represents your life path. The crossing line is the gateway, portal, or doorway. The two small lines represent time and space. These two aspects help create the doorway. They are also markers for the mind to let go of these concepts. As you pass through the gateway the path fades away. This is the expansion point.

    I have used this symbol as a personal journey in meditation. This symbol has also been used for healing, manifesting, and as a focal point to get centered and find peace. Please play with this symbol and let yourself be guided on how best to use it for yourself.

The Expanded Gateway Vol. 2

Wisdom for the Awakened Cosciouness

Fairy Wisdom
Part 2

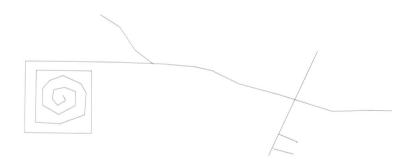

Home is a feeling of peace. Where do you feel at home? This could be a place, a relationship, or even just a moment in time. Is there a longing for home or does it live in your heart?

Love is not just about giving, you also must allow yourself to be vulnerable enough to receive. Often Humanity focuses on the giving of love. This is a very important aspect of love, but it is only half of it. Love is a cycle, or a flow, and it must go both directions to create a relationship.

Gratitude is the best way to open and ask for more. When you give thanks for all that you already have you signal the Universe that you would like more of that goodness. Gratitude is not about be undeserving or humbling yourself. It is an act of celebration. It is asking the Universe to party with you.

You are never alone. Ask for help and keep asking for help as you need it. The trick is to also accept the help when it arrives. Being alone does not make you strong. You become stronger by allowing us, The One, and other Humans to support you. It is love that makes Humanity stronger.

Spellbound. Humanity defines this as frozen or obsessed. We Fairies define it as focused intention. What will you let spellbound you today? Is it what you want your focus to be? You do not have to be frozen or stuck in a focus you do not want. Make sure you are choosing your focus.

Acceptance is the key to moving forward. Accept everything including yourself as it is in this moment. This doesn't mean you agree with it, just that you stop resisting it. Acceptance allows for new solutions to appear. acceptance means you lay down your sword, open your eyes, and embrace what you find there.

The laws of the universe are simple. Magic is simple. Do not let your mind create more steps then you need to do it. Ask for an answer or solution and then receive it. You can do a complicated dance or walk a straight line, but both will get you from one point to another. How do you want to experience the journey?

Look for the need that is living in your soul. Listen to the whispers in your mind. Feel your greatness. Humanity creates from need not want. Whatever your soul believes it needs to survive it will create. When your soul is longing for something you will keep creating the opportunity for that experience.

Be

Here

Now

Life is happening. It is your feelings, reactions, and judgments that make it good or bad. If you can allow yourself to experience without all your filters then your perspective will change.

When you open to the unexplained and allow the unexpected you open to solutions and answers you weren't open to before. Humanity always wants to understand with their mind. We would like you to instead feel with your heart. Rational thought can only get you so far.

There is no end. Goals are just sign posts on a longer journey. There is no finish line. Even death is just another part if your soul's journey. There is never a time when everything will be complete and you will be done. Please stop trying to "get through" events, times, or life. Allow moments to soak in, experiences to unfold, and your soul to evolve.

Divine timing is not your timing. Life is happening at its own speed. Trying to push or pull it will just bring you frustration. Accept the Divine flows pace and find peace.

You are a creator, an artist, and a thinker of thoughts. It is a delicate dance to mold something into being without destroying it in the process. Give your inspiration the breath of life and then room to breathe. A tight grip can suffocate the spark.

How much is your time worth? How about your art, your words, your life, or your soul? You set the value of your actions, words, and gifts. Do not give this authority away. There is always an exchange in every interaction or relationship. Be aware of how much you are giving and how much you are receiving. there must be balance.

Bring your focus to this moment. feel, see, hear, taste, and sense all of now. When you are fully present with this moment your mind cannot worry, stress, or be in fear about the future or the past.

Wisdom for the Awakened Cosciouness

Manifesting Exercises

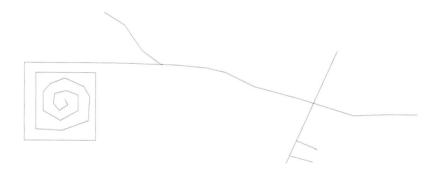

There are two manifesting exercises that I would like to share with you. One is from the Fairies. It involves planting the seed of intention and releasing it to the Fairies and the universe for manifestation. The other is using the E.L.F.E. symbol to pull what you need from the ethers and into the physical. Both of these I do as visualizations or meditations. Allow yourself to play with them and find what works best for you. You might find drawing them on paper or acting them out works better for you. Everyone's energy is different and need different visual cues and practices.

The Manifesting Fairy Flower

Manifesting comes from a need for a particular feeling. When we want to manifest physical things we are looking for a feeling of safety or joy or pleasure. So, this exercise starts off with figuring out what you want to manifest and the feeling you are trying to create with it. Once you have that feeling and the physical thing you would like to manifest (this can be an event, thing, relationship, etc.) and placing them into a seed (in your mind). The next part involves the chakra system. Chakra's are energy centers in the center of your being. The first chakra, or root chakra, sits down in between your pelvic bone and tail bone. The next is behind you belly button, and the third is right under your rib cage. The heart chakra is your fourth chakra and the fifth is your throat. The last two chakras are your third eye and your crown at the top of your head. There is a lot of information in books and on the internet about chakras and the chakra system so please feel free to research and find out more. There is way too much to fit in a small book like this and it is not necessary for this exercise.

To do the exercise get in a comfortable place and relax your body. Now see the seed holding the energy of your intention. You are going to place it in the fertile ground that lives in your root chakra. Let the energy sit there and begin to sprout. See the roots going deep into the earth. Then notice the sprout starting to rise up out of the ground. Experience it as the plant grows up into the second chakra (behind the belly button) and let it rest there for a minute. See if there are any emotions that needs to release. Allow them to rise and release. Then watch the plant rise up into the third chakra. Let it rest there a minute. Again, if there are any emotions that feel like might block the plant, acknowledge them and let them release. Now the plant will be rising up into your heart chakra. Let it rest here and be showered by love. Allow the love to rain down and wash it clean. Next the plant will grow up into your throat. Let it push through and open the pathways for your expression of this manifestation. Experience the plant as it spreads up into your third eye. Here it will open your intuition to what you need to know for your manifestation. Lastly it will grow into your crown chakra. Here you will see it blossom. It may bare fruit or flower or just have giant leaves. Now pluck this fruition and hand it over to the Fairies that are nearby. Let the Fairies magically change this fruition into energy. This energy now flows down into your physical body and allow it to harmonize with all of your cells. Now give thanks for the manifestation of this intention. Gratitude for its realization helps the energy manifest that much quicker. Now thank the Fairies for all their help.

E.L.F.E. Manifestation

This exercise starts by visualizing the E.L.F.E. symbol mirrored path end to path end. It looks like this

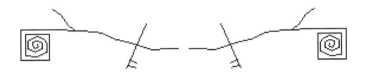

Now visualize what ever you want to manifest in the center of the spiral on the right. This represents the center of the universe or the ethers. You are then going to see this travel along the lines as if it was following a path. As it passes through the first gateway the breath of life enters the intention. The witness it travel through the second gateway point into the physical realm. Watch as it continues into the spiral. The spiral represents your physical world, or your heart, or both. Once the intention reaches the end of the spiral experience it dispersing as energy into every cell of your physical body. It now lives as a physical energy within you and you can attract it in easily.

Fairy Wisdom
Part 3

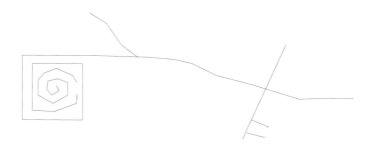

Laugh, giggle, and snort. Let yourself be silly. It is time to play! Give your worry and stress a break. Your mind needs fun to function properly. Make sure to find the value of play and goofy moments.

When inspiration hits you can react in two ways. You can strike fast while the iron is hot or you can let it simmer on a low boil. It all depends on the inspiration. Let yourself be guided to the correct action for you.

You can find love and joy in every moment. It will either be there for you to receive or time for you to share it. These energies are always accessible. Let us show you.

Take a moment to think about how awesome you are. Awesome means to inspire awe. There are many people waiting for you to inspire them. Let your magic be expressed clearly to those that need to experience it.

Connect with those who align you with joy and peace. A simple conversation can shift your whole day. The right kind of people in your life can shift your whole life.

Fear comes from a feeling of lack. The best way out of fear is through gratitude. Gratitude is the path to abundance. This can be a lack of love, money, peace, personal space, or time. There is an abundance of all these energies in the world. Express gratitude for the places they already are in your life.

Your heart and soul are always telling you want you are longing for. You just need to stop and listen. When you quiet your mind it gives your heart the space to be heard. You will notice subtle signs all around you.

You may think you know what you need or want but the Universe may have a much better solution. Open to it. You will be guided. Take the little steps you can. They will build into something bigger and better then you ever dreamed.

You are a creator. You create with your thoughts and your actions. Worry is created by assumptions about the future. Hope is created by being open to the future.

Focus on this moment, this step, this action, and let the rest fall away. The past is done. The future is unfolding. When your mind is present in the here and now you can see things clearly.

Many in Humanity think they cannot accept something but the truth often is they don't understand. They don't understand the reason behind a "tragedy". They don't think the guidance they have received makes sense. They don't see where their path is leading them. Accepting and understanding are completely different things. Try to accept even if you don't understand. Don't let your desire to understand keep you from the answer.

Trust the Universe to bring you solutions and be willing to change. that is co-creation. setting your intention and allowing it to take form in Divine timing. that is co-creation. Let your manifestation finish coking. Wait till it is golden brown and then let it cool.

I trust

My body

The Universe

Love

Pleasure

and Joy

When you try to push the energy, or pull the energy, you are stuck in a power struggle. When you surrender to the energy that is present, and see where it is leading you, what seems stuck becomes unstuck.

If you are feeling overwhelmed you are trying to control too much. Trust and let go. When you feel crazy, sad, stressed, or afraid, focus on the now. Be here now. Soon this will all change. When you accept and love now, you find peace and joy.

You judge yourself too harshly. Others' judgments come from their own feelings of lack or fear for you. Do not let their perceptions color your experience. Spend today and everyday being love.

ABOUT THE AUTHOR

Elizabeth Saenz is also the author of The Expanded Gateway: Messages to Expand Your Consciousness (vol.1), The Fairy wisdom Oracle, Fairy Tid-bits, and "The Fairies and Me" Blog. In her business, The Expanded Gateway, she has helped hundreds become empowered and connect to their spiritual guides using her talents as a Reiki Master, ThetaHealer, ordained minister, channel, and intuitive. She has been talking to the Fairies and other guides all her life. This life-experience has led her to act as a representative for The Fairy Realm on Earth. She lives on Whidbey Island in Washington State with her husband and three beautiful children.